W9-BLR-554

The KidHaven Science Library

Molds and Fungi

by Buffy Silverman

KIDHAVEN PRESS

An imprint of Thomson Gale, a part of The Thomson Corporation

San Diego • Detroit • New York • San Francisco • Cleveland
New Haven, Conn. • Waterville, Maine • London • Munich

For more information, contact
KidHaven Press
27500 Drake Rd.
Farmington Hills, MI 48331-3535
Or you can visit our Internet site at http://www.gale.com

LIBRARY OF CONGRESS CATALOGING-IN-PUBLICATION DATA

Silverman, Buffy.
Molds and fungi / by Buffy Silverman.
p. cm. — (The Kidhaven science library)
Includes bibliographical references and index.
ISBN 0-7377-2075-1
1. Molds (Fungi)—Juvenile literature. 2. Fungi—Juvenile literature. [1. Molds (Fungi) 2. Fungi.] I. Title. II. Series.
QK603.5.S526 2004
579.5—dc22

2003023377

Printed in the United States of America

Contents

Chapter 1
What Are Molds and Fungi? 4

Chapter 2
The Variety of Fungi 12

Chapter 3
Fungi and the Food Chain 22

Chapter 4
Fungi and People 31

Glossary 41

For Further Exploration 43

Index 45

Picture Credits 47

About the Author 48

What Are Molds and Fungi?

Mold is the common name given to a wide variety of fungi. The black, fuzzy mold that grows on bread is a kind of fungus. Molds growing in damp basements are fungi. Blue and green molds and water molds are types of fungi.

Fungi live all over the world. They grow in warm tropical rain forests, on the frozen Arctic tundra, in lakes and rivers, and in oceans.

Many fungi grow on dead things, like leaves, logs, or dead animals. Because dead plants and animals fall to the ground, fungi are often found in the soil. Other fungi live on living plants and animals, including people.

Some fungi are so small that they can only be seen with a microscope. Other fungi grow larger than a football field. Fungi come in all colors: red, yellow, black, white, blue, purple, green, and orange.

Despite the amazing variety of fungi, all are alike in important ways. Under a microscope, all fungi have certain features that are the same.

Scientists estimate that there are more than a million species of fungi growing all over the world.

The Kingdom Fungi

Scientists group living things to show how they are related to one another. Fungi make up one **kingdom**. Green plants belong to another kingdom. Animals make up a third kingdom. The other kingdoms contain microscopic organisms, like bacteria.

All of the living things in a kingdom share certain characteristics. For example, all of the living things in the fungi kingdom get their food in the same way and are made of cells with similar features. Within a kingdom, living things are further grouped. Fungi are grouped by the way they make spores when they reproduce.

When scientists study a living thing, they give it a scientific name. Every kind of fungus is given a unique scientific name. Scientists have studied and named about two hundred thousand different kinds of fungi. They estimate that over 1 million species of fungi live on the earth.

The Fungus Body

A fungus is made up of **cells**. Cells are so small that they can only be seen with a microscope. The cells of fungi are different from animal, plant, or bacteria cells. Unlike bacteria, a fungus cell has a nucleus that controls the cell. Plant and animal cells also have nuclei. Unlike animal cells, a fungus cell has a stiff cell wall around it. Although plant cells also have cell walls, they are made of a different chemical. Plant cell walls are made of cellulose. The cell walls of fungi are made of **chitin**, the same chemical found in the hard shells of insects.

A fungus has a simple body. Unlike a plant, it has no roots, stems, or leaves. It does not have tubes inside its body to carry nutrients to different parts. Instead, a fungus is made of small white threads, called **hyphae**. The fungus grows as each thread gets

Some fungi are black but many fungi come in bright colors like purple, orange, or yellow.

longer and longer, then branches and makes new threads. The hyphae grow in all directions, and cover more area. The hyphae grow over material that is food for fungi.

A large colony of these white threads is called a **mycelium**. A mycelium is the whole body of a single fungus. Usually a mycelium forms a mat underground, or in a dead log, a piece of bread, or other food source. Some mycelia can grow for many years. Scientists studying fungi in northern Michigan, for example, found a single mycelium that had spread

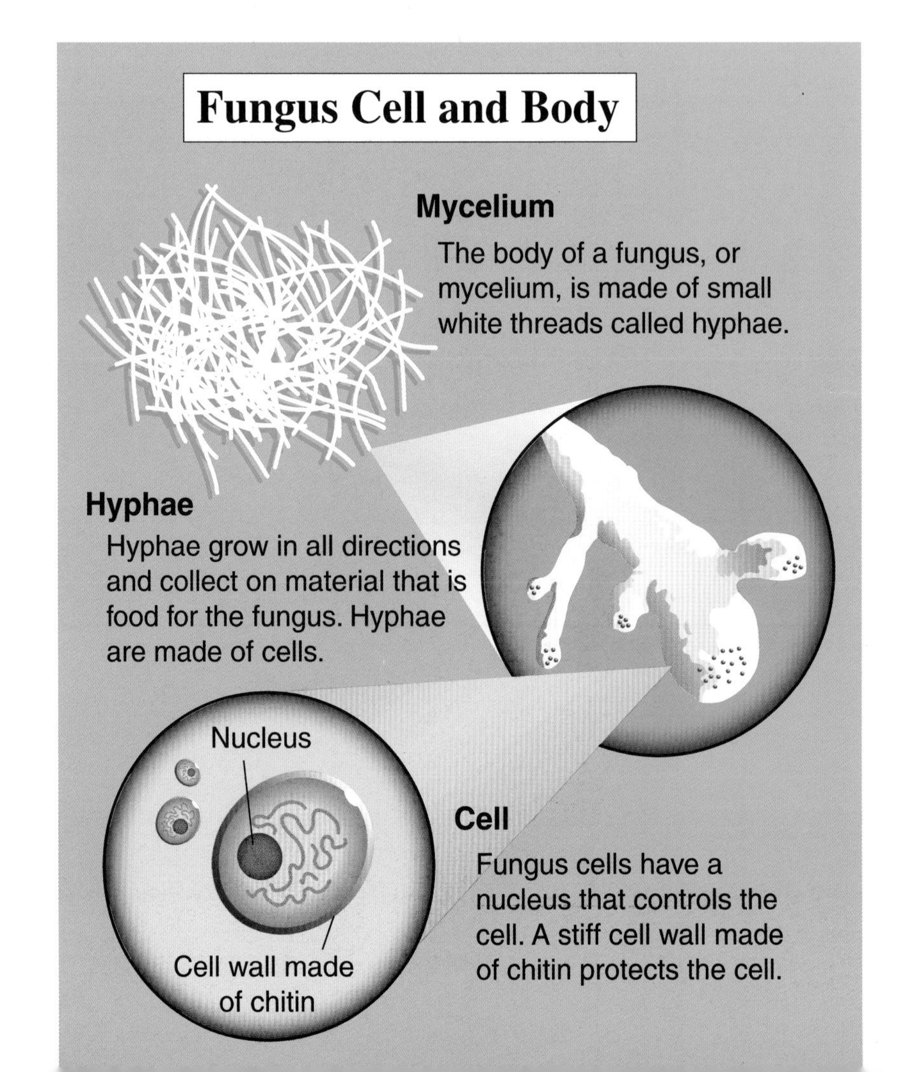

over a thirty-five-acre woodland. They estimated that it was fifteen hundred years old.

Food for Fungi

Like all living things, fungi need energy from food to grow and reproduce. Fungi get their food by eating other plants and animals. Fungi digest their food before taking it inside their bodies. Fungi make special chemicals, called **enzymes**, that break down their food.

Enzymes ooze out of a fungus onto dead leaves. The enzymes break the leaves into smaller compounds that dissolve in water. Then the fungus absorbs water and food, giving it energy to live and grow.

Spores

When fungi reproduce, they make **spores** that can travel through air or water. If a spore lands on a place where there is food, water, and space, it can germinate and grow into a new fungus.

Some fungi grow spores on the tips of hyphae. Others grow special structures, called fruiting bodies, which make huge quantities of spores.

A **mushroom** is a kind of fruiting body that makes spores. A mushroom has a long stalk and an umbrella-shaped cap. Under the cap are hundreds of thin sheets, called **gills**, that are arranged like bicycle spokes. Spores grow on club-shaped

Gills are arranged like bicycle spokes under a mushroom cap. This is where the reproductive spores grow.

structures on the gills. One mushroom contains millions and millions of spores.

A bracket fungus is another kind of fruiting body with spores growing inside. Instead of gills, a bracket fungus has tubes where it makes spores. The spores fall from tiny openings on the bottom of the bracket, called **pores.**

Spores come in all colors, shapes, and sizes. Many spores are only a single cell, and are too small to be seen without a microscope. Even though fungi spores do not look alike, they are all designed to move to a new place and grow into a new fungus. Some fruiting bodies are made to shoot spores into the air so they will travel away from a fungus. Many fruiting bodies drop their spores and rely on the wind to move them. Other spores float to new places on water. Animals carry spores from place to place.

From Spore to Fungus

Because spores are tiny and lightweight, they drift in the wind. Spores can travel over one thousand miles before landing and germinating. Most spores, however, do not land in a place where they can grow.

By making many, many spores, a fungus increases the chances that a few will grow into new fungi. For example, a fungus called smut grows on corn. It produces 25 billion spores per ear of corn.

A spore can survive for a long time before germinating and growing into a new fungus. If temperatures are too hot or cold, or if there is not enough moisture, a spore does not germinate. When conditions are right, a spore swells and a hypha starts to grow. If the hypha comes in contact with food, it can get energy and grow into a new fungus.

Fungi are simple living things that provide an essential service to all living things. By breaking down and consuming dead matter, fungi help all other living things.

Chapter 2

The Variety of Fungi

Fungi grow everywhere. Hidden in soil, wood, and other material are the mycelia of many kinds of fungi. A huge variety of fungi live around the globe.

Fairy Rings

When a fungus spore germinates, it grows hyphae in all directions. As a mycelium grows, the older hyphae in the center use the available food and die. New hyphae continue to grow outward, forming a circle.

Fairy ring fungi grow underground, in a lawn. They form a circle-shaped mycelium, with the living, growing hyphae on the outer edge of the circle. Because the fairy ring mycelium uses **nutrients** in the soil, the grass inside the fairy ring is yellow and unhealthy.

About once a year, when the ground is warm and moist, knots of hyphae swell along the growing edge of the mycelium. These hyphae sprout into a circle of mushrooms. Each mushroom contains millions of spores that drift in the wind. A few spores land where there is food and grow into new fairy rings.

The mushrooms soon die, but the mycelium continues to grow. Fairy rings grow slowly, about eight inches a year. But they keep growing and growing. A fairy ring mycelium grows outward until it reaches a place where it cannot get food. Often the mycelium grows to a diameter of over thirty feet. One fairy ring in France is almost a half-mile across and has been growing for about seven hundred years.

Long ago people thought fairy rings occurred when fairies danced on grass, trampling it and turning it yellow. They believed that fairies, elves, and

Fairy ring fungi spend most of the time growing underground. About once a year they sprout into a circle of mushrooms on a lawn.

goblins sat on the circle of mushrooms, watching the dancers.

Puffballs

A puffball's mycelium grows underground or in rotting wood. It sprouts pear-shaped balls, called puffballs, that grow spores. These spongy balls dry when they age. As it ripens, a white puffball darkens, and an opening forms on its top. Clouds of brown spores escape through the opening. Raindrops splashing on a puffball cause it to puff out spores, which are carried by the wind. A person or animal stepping on a puffball also makes it release a smoky cloud of spores.

Common puffballs grow to be about the size of a golf ball. Another kind of puffball, called the giant puffball, grows to the size of a pumpkin or even larger. People have mistaken giant puffballs in pastures for sheep, since they can grow to be the same size and are the same color. A giant puffball can contain 7 trillion spores. When it cracks open, the wind carries its spores.

The spores of a giant puffball are like a fine powder. Native Americans once used puffball spores to treat wounds. The spores slowed bleeding and helped blood to clot.

Earthstars

The fruiting body of an earthstar is shaped like an onion and covered with layers of skin. When it rains,

When raindrops strike a puffball, a thick cloud of spores escapes through the opening on the top.

the outer layers split and peel back like a banana, forming a star. Inside the star is a sac that contains spores and resembles a puffball.

As a star curls back, it raises the sac. The rays of some earthstars raise the sac four inches above the surrounding leaves and soil. This puts the sac in a place where its spores can be carried by the wind. Raindrops hit the sac, causing spores to puff out through an opening on the top.

Bracket Fungi

Although their mycelia remain alive, mushrooms and many other fruiting bodies dry up and disappear after a short time. But bracket fungi make fruiting bodies that last for months or years.

Bracket fungi grow on trees and stumps. Their mycelia penetrate inside a tree and get nourishment from the tree. By feeding on a tree, bracket fungi can harm a living tree or break down a dead one.

Bird's Nest Fungi

Bird's nest fungi grow on rotting logs. They make little packets of spores inside a cup. The spore packets look like eggs in a bird's nest.

The spore packets are too big and heavy to be lifted out of the cup by the wind. When it rains, however, the spore packets can escape their nest. A falling raindrop hits a spore packet and splashes it over the side of the cup. Sometimes the packets get stuck on

Bracket fungi can live for years by getting nourishment from inside a living tree or even a dead stump.

a nearby stick or blade of grass. Eventually the cover of the spore packet wears off, and its spores are released.

Stinkhorn Fungi

Stinkhorn fungi depend on animals to move their spores. They attract flies by making an odor that smells like rotting meat.

A stinkhorn mycelium feeds on decaying leaves in a forest. When growing conditions are right, the hyphae form a structure that is the size and shape of a chicken's egg. Within a few hours the egg "hatches." It expands to a long white stalk, with a dark slimy cap.

The stinky cap has spores in the slime. When a fly lands on the cap, the slime and spores stick to its

In France, Italy, and Germany, people use pigs to sniff out truffles, a rare and expensive delicacy.

body. The fly carries spores away. Some spores fall off the fly and grow into new fungi.

Truffles

One of the fungi people like to eat is truffles. Truffle fungi grow underground, on the roots of trees, in France, Germany, and Italy.

The fruiting bodies also grow underground and make a strong odor. The spores are spread with the help of animals. When squirrels and chipmunks smell truffles, they dig them up for food and some spores drift away.

People use trained pigs and dogs to hunt truffles. After an animal sniffs out truffles, its owner pulls the animal away. Then the person carefully digs up the truffles.

People find fewer truffles today than they did one hundred years ago. Many forests have been cut down, and air pollution has harmed trees. Because truffles are uncommon and hard to find, they are very expensive. Truffles have sold for four hundred dollars an ounce. At that price a pound of truffles costs sixty-four hundred dollars!

Morels

In the spring, mushroom hunters in North America head to the woods to search for morels. Morels do not have gills under their caps. The cap of a morel is covered in pits, resembling a brain. Spores form in sacs in the pits.

Morels often grow in the same spot, year after year. When mushroom hunters find morels, they try to keep the location a secret and return to the spot each spring.

Morels are safe to eat. But some people confuse them with a similar mushroom, called false morels.

False morels also grow in woods in the springtime, and can poison or kill a person.

Yeasts

Although yeasts are fungi, most do not have hyphae or mycelia. Yeast is made of a single cell and can only be seen with a microscope. There are hundreds of different yeasts.

People have used yeast for thousands of years for baking bread and making wine. When yeast cells

Fungi grow when spores, like these which have gathered in the form of a cap, settle out of the air and land on food.

digest sugar, they make bubbles of carbon dioxide. These bubbles make bread rise. Yeasts also produce alcohol when they digest sugar, turning grapes into wine.

Bread Molds

Billions and billions of fungi spores float in the air. Inside every building there are spores. One of the most common fungi found in a home is a black mold.

The mold spores settle out of the air and land everywhere in a home. Most of the spores do not grow into molds because they do not land where there are food and moisture. But some spores do land on food and grow.

Spores that land on a moist slice of bread germinate and grow into hyphae. The hyphae grow inside the bread and form a thick white mycelium. Some hyphae grow upright on the surface of the bread. On top of these hyphae, tiny capsules of spores form. When the spores are ripe, the capsules split open. Millions of new spores are released into the air.

Although bread molds do not resemble fairy rings, truffles, yeasts, or other fungi, they are alike in important ways: They break down materials and make spores that grow into new fungi.

Fungi have an almost endless variety of shapes and types. No matter what kind of shape they have, fungi all provide an essential service to life on earth.

Chapter 3

Fungi and the Food Chain

All fungi break down their food with enzymes, then absorb it. Although the way that fungi get food is the same, different fungi use different types of foods.

Recyclers

Most fungi live off dead or decaying food. They consume dead plants, animals, and microorganisms. Fungi that eat dead or decaying matter are called **saprophytes** or **decomposers**.

Many different fungi consume fallen leaves and rotting logs. Their hyphae penetrate leaves. Enzymes from fungi break down leaves into smaller and smaller pieces. Fungi use some of the material in leaves so they can live and grow. Some of the chemicals in leaves are dissolved by rainwater and wash into the soil. Earthworms and other soil animals mix tiny leaf fragments and minerals that fungi produce. The organic matter and chemicals that are mixed into the soil enrich it so plants can grow.

Decomposers release carbon dioxide, nitrates, and other chemicals into soil, water, and air. Plants cannot live and grow without the chemicals that fungi release when they break down their food. Animals that consume plants depend on plants for their energy. Animals that eat animals also depend on growing plants, since they eat animals that eat plants. Thus plants and animals need fungi that are decomposers.

The speed at which fungi decompose dead plants and animals depends on several factors. Fungi need oxygen to grow and consume food. When there is little oxygen, fungi grow slowly, and decomposition

A thick layer of green mold grows on a loaf of bread.

is slow. Fungi also need moisture for growth. If temperatures are too high or too low, fungi do not grow, and decomposition slows. If their food source does not have important minerals, like nitrogen, fungal growth also slows.

Different fungi recycle different things. Some decompose only one type of food, like branches, logs, or stumps. Others eat many different kinds of organisms. There are fungi that live on dead animals and animal wastes. Some consume cardboard

Decomposer fungi eat dead or decaying matter such as rotting logs or fallen leaves.

boxes or wooden buildings. Fungi decompose glue, clothing, and paint. There are even fungi that attack jet fuel. Fungi decompose anything made from living things.

Parasites

Fungi that get their energy from living plants and animals are called **parasites**. The plants or animals they consume are called their host. Some fungi are parasites on other fungi.

Some parasitic fungi attack only one kind of plant or animal. Other parasites live on many different hosts. Fungi that are decomposers can also be parasites; many feed on both dead and living organisms.

In certain conditions, parasitic fungi can spread like wildfire. This is often true when a fungus is introduced into a new habitat where it has no natural enemies. For example, one fungus caused a disease called chestnut blight.

The fungus grew on Oriental chestnut trees in Asia, but did not damage those trees. Oriental chestnut trees were brought to North America from Japan and planted in parks. The fungus came with them to North America. Spores of the fungus filled the air and started growing on nearby American chestnut trees.

In 1904, a forester from the New York City Zoological Park in the Bronx noticed that a few American chestnut trees were infected with chestnut blight. Within a year, almost every American

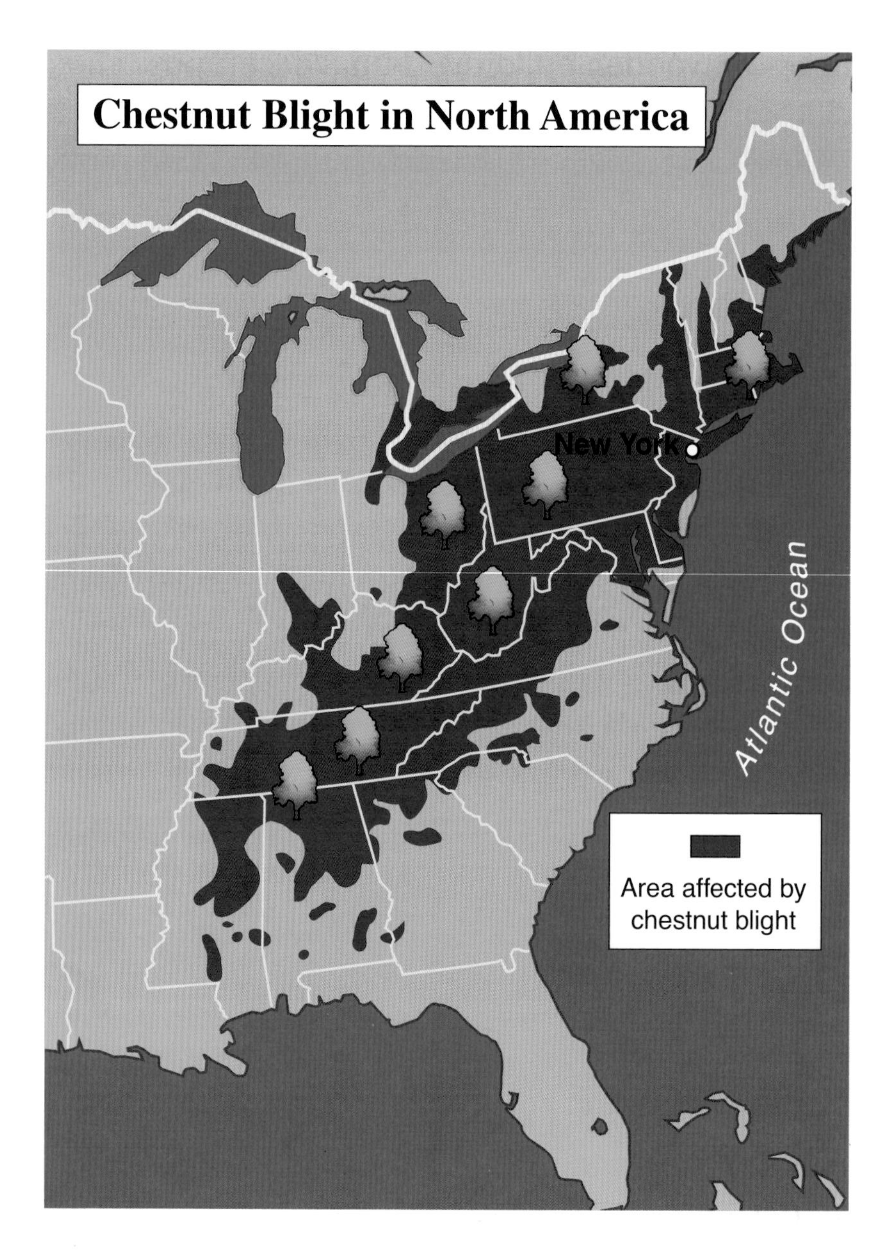

chestnut tree in the Bronx had chestnut blight, and the disease started killing the trees.

The fungus's spores oozed out in sticky, gooey masses that stuck to squirrels and birds. The animals spread the fungus when they traveled to other chestnut trees. Within fifty years the fungus had killed all the American chestnut trees. Because the fungus did not harm the trees' roots, new trees sprouted. But those trees were killed by chestnut blight by the time they reached twenty feet tall. Scientists hope to return American chestnut trees to eastern forests by breeding them with disease-resistant Oriental trees.

People have learned to control some parasitic fungi. Some fungi can be controlled with chemicals, called **fungicides**, which kill parasitic fungi and stop the damage.

People also use parasitic fungi to control insect pests. There are many fungi that eat insects. The spores of these fungi can be used to reduce the numbers of insects that attack crops. Colorado potato beetles, spittlebugs, leafhoppers, and other insect pests are now controlled with parasitic fungi.

Mutualists

Some fungi that live with a plant or animal help their host. Many fungi help the plants that nourish them get minerals and water from the soil or the air. Other fungi are nourished by animals that "farm" them. When both partners benefit from living together, they are called **mutualists**.

Most plants have fungi living on their roots. Pine, beech, oak, and birch trees have fungi covering the outside of their roots. The hyphae of these fungi branch and penetrate a large area of soil, helping the tree roots soak up more water and minerals. In exchange, the trees supply the fungi with sugars that they make. Truffles are one of the many fungi that live on the outside of tree roots.

Many other plants, including grasses, shrubs, and some trees, have fungi on their roots that grow right into the root cells. These fungi absorb up to one-fourth of the food that the plants make. However, the plants grow better than they could without the fungi. The fungi help them absorb enough water and minerals and protect them from parasites in the soil.

Some fungi live with algae on rocks, tree bark, and in the soil of deserts, mountains, and the northern tundra. Partnerships of fungi and algae are called **lichens.** Although algae normally live in lakes and ponds, they can survive in harsh environments with the help of fungi. The fungi keep the algae from drying out and absorb water quickly from the soil and air. Tough hyphae surround the algae, protecting them from plant eaters. In exchange, the algae give the fungi from 40 to 90 percent of the sugar they make. Neither the fungi nor algae could survive on their own.

Fungi Farmers

Certain ants, termites, and beetles "farm" fungi. Leaf-cutting ants in Central and South America

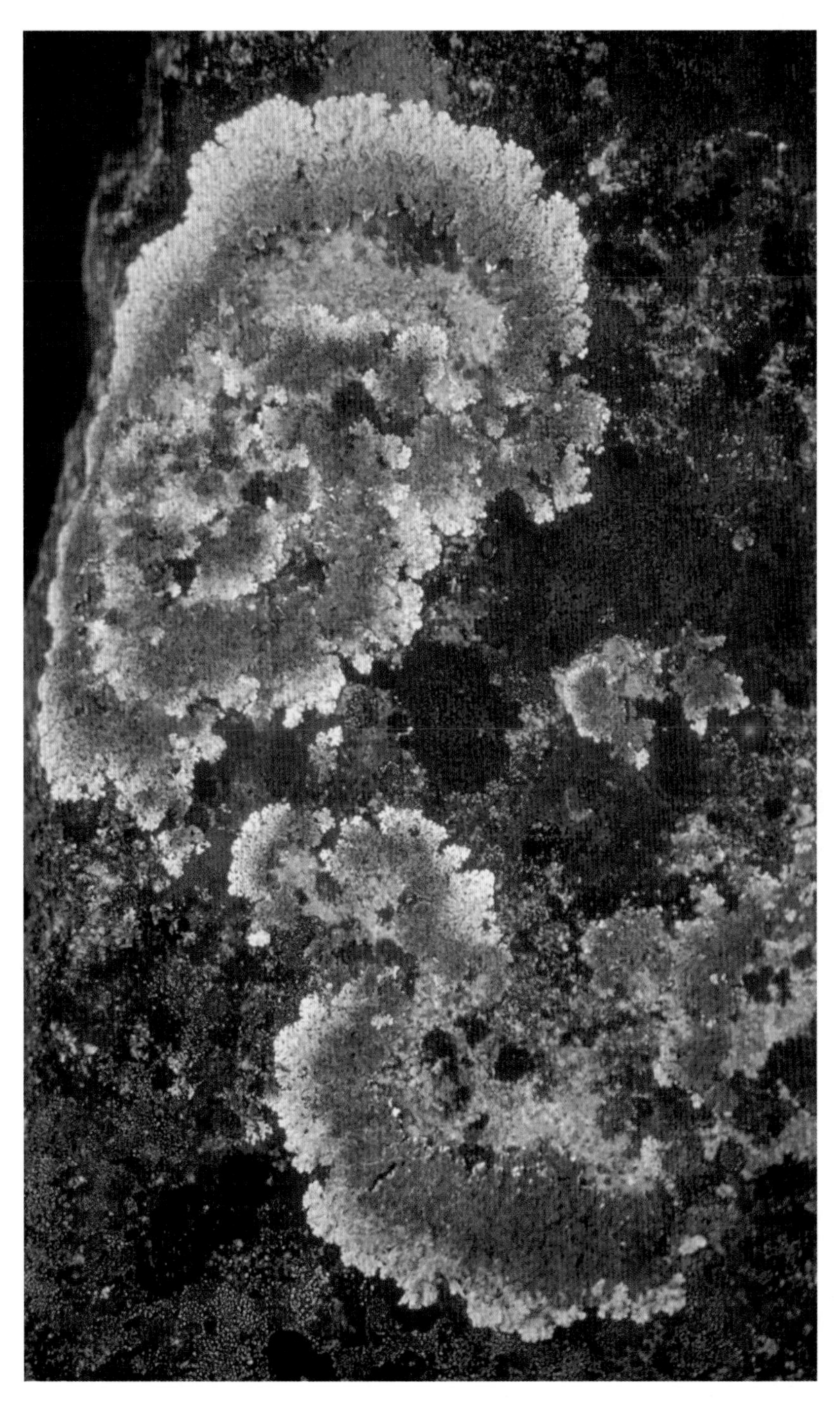

Lichens form when algae and fungi work together.

All fungi, such as these mushrooms, play an important role in the environment.

raise fungus gardens in underground nests. Worker ants cut pieces of leaves and carry them to the nest. Other workers chew the leaf pieces and mix them with saliva. On the leaf paste they place bits of fungi hyphae, which grow into a mat of mycelium. The workers patrol their gardens and remove other invading fungi. When the fungi produce swollen hyphae, the workers harvest them. If they were not harvested, the swollen hyphae would grow into mushrooms. The hyphae are fed to both young and adult ants. The young ants need the fungi to grow. The fungi need the leaf fragments for food.

Whether decomposers, parasites, or mutualists, all fungi play an important role in the environment. They decompose dead material so there are space and nutrients for new life. Some fungi harm plants and animals, whereas others help living things.

Fungi and People

Wherever people live, fungi live too. Some fungi harm people by causing diseases or making poisonous chemicals. Others harm the plants and animals that people depend on for food. There are fungi that rot and contaminate human food. Some destroy buildings, clothing, and other things that people make.

Other fungi help people. All animals, including people, depend on fungi to decompose and recycle dead organisms. For thousands of years people have used fungi to bake bread, make wine and beer, and manufacture some cheeses. People eat many fungi. People have also discovered important fungi-derived medicines that cure human diseases and save lives.

Plant Diseases

Many parasitic fungi harm the plants people grow. People have been aware of plant diseases since they began farming. Wheat, oats, barley, and rye were some of the first crops people grew. All of these crops got diseases caused by rust fungi.

Fungi can rot or contaminate food as can be seen with this strawberry.

But it was not until the late 1800s that people understood that fungi caused many plant diseases. Before that, diseases were seen as the devil's work or the result of other unseen forces.

When European explorers collected crops from around the world, they were not aware that they also brought back parasitic fungi. In the 1500s, Spanish explorers introduced potatoes from South America. European peasants found that, by planting potatoes, they could grow enough food to survive all year. Potatoes were easy to grow and produced lots of food on a small plot of land. Because of this, potatoes became the most important crop in Ireland. By the late 1700s, a typical Irish family ate 250 pounds of potatoes a week and little else.

In the summers of 1845 and 1846, the weather in Ireland and the rest of Europe was unusually cool and wet. This weather was perfect for the spread of *Phytophthora infestans*, a fungus that causes a disease called potato blight. For two years, black spots covered the leaves and stems of potato plants, killing them and rotting the underground potatoes.

In this picture, potato blight covers the plant's leaves (right), kills the potatoes (bottom), and makes the plant helpless against bugs and pests.

Because potatoes were the only food for many Irish people, over 1 million people starved and died. Many others were weak and became ill. More than 2 million people left Ireland, most of them going to North America.

In 1861 a scientist named Anton DeBary showed that a fungus caused the potato blight. He found that the hyphae of the fungus spent the winter in old potato plants with diseased leaves or stems. Farmers piled old plants on the sides of fields where they grew potatoes. In the spring, fungi spores blew from these piles onto new potato plants and infected them. Scientists later discovered that, by applying copper sulfate, they could stop the potato blight. Today the fungus still causes $4 billion of damage to potato crops around the world.

Human Diseases

Over fifty different fungi are known to cause human diseases. Many of these fungi grow on people's skin, causing rashes. These fungi live in the soil, but they can also grow on hair, skin, and feathers. They can live on a person's nails or on the lens of an eye.

Athlete's foot and ringworm are two common skin diseases caused by fungi. Fungi thrive under tightly fitting clothing and shoes where they find a warm, moist environment. By applying a cream containing fungicide, people can control these infections.

In 1928, Alexander Fleming discovered penicillin, a mold that stopped the growth of germs.

Molds and Medicines

Although some fungi cause diseases, other fungi cure human and animal illnesses. Until the 1940s people commonly died because bacteria grew in scratches or wounds. But after the discovery of **penicillin**, developed from a mold, bacterial infections were easily cured.

In 1928, Dr. Alexander Fleming, a British scientist, was studying bacteria that caused human diseases.

At his lab, Fleming grew bacteria in petri dishes. One day he noticed that a mold had contaminated one of his dishes. There were no bacteria growing around the mold. Fleming suspected that the mold made a chemical that killed the bacteria.

Fleming published a paper describing a substance he called penicillin. Penicillin was made by the mold, *Penicillium notatum*. Fleming discovered that penicillin stopped the growth of germs.

Other scientists began growing and purifying penicillin from molds. During World War II, scientists raced to discover how to grow the mold and make enough penicillin to use as a drug. They were trying to save soldiers who were dying from infections from wounds.

Antibiotics

In 1943, Mary Hunt brought a moldy cantaloupe to the laboratory where she worked in Peoria, Illinois. This *Penicillium* mold grew very fast in a laboratory tank. Scientists were finally able to make enough penicillin to use it as a drug. Penicillin was the first **antibiotic**, a drug that can kill bacteria.

Recently scientists have found new drugs made by fungi. Several different molds make chemicals called cyclosporins. When someone has an organ transplant, the person is given cyclosporin. This drug stops a person's body from rejecting the new organ. People with diabetes have also been treated with cyclosporin.

Because fungi produce so many chemicals, scientists believe they will discover more drugs that may improve human life. Some fungi have been used in Chinese and Japanese medicine for thousands of years. Scientists are now studying these and other fungi.

Penicillin, shown magnified (right), comes from mold that scientists grow in a laboratory (below).

The Future of Fungi

Just as fungi have a large impact on people and all other living things, people have an impact on fungi. When people clear land for roads, buildings, and farming, they destroy fungi mycelia. Many fungi grow underground where they are not seen. The effect of human activity on fungi is often not considered.

People have cleared huge sections of tropical rain forest for farming and lumber. Because tropical forests have lush vegetation, farmers thought that they could grow crops where tropical trees once stood. However, they found that crops could not grow for long in tropical soils. After a few years, another plot of forest had to be cleared.

Biologists now understand that tropical forests are not like the forests of temperate climates. There is not a thick layer of rich soil under plants. Instead there is a thin layer of rotting leaves and fruit. Leaves, branches, and other dead matter constantly fall to the ground.

Beneath the rotting leaves are dense mats of fungi mycelia. These fungi are connected to the roots of tropical trees. Tree roots depend on the fungi to get enough water and nutrients from the soil. The fungi decompose whatever falls to the ground and recycle nutrients. When tropical forests are cleared, there is no plant debris for fungi to consume. They die in the hot sun. Without fungi, tropical soils do not have enough nutrients for growing plants.

Tropical forests are not the only places where fungi are declining. European biologists have noticed a decline in wild mushrooms in recent years. Scientists are not sure why fewer mushrooms are growing. Some think that chemical fertilizers on nearby farms might harm fungi. They have also noticed that some trees in European forests are dying. They worry that trees are not able to get the

As people cut down tropical forests for farming and lumber, fungi die and tropical soils no longer have enough nutrients for growing plants.

Scientists think that chemical fertilizers used on many farms may harm mushrooms and other fungi growing in the forest.

water and nutrients they need to grow because there are fewer fungi growing on tree roots.

When people protect forests and other natural habitats, they also protect the fungi that grow there. Like all living things, fungi need clean water and air and a place to grow. Fungi are a necessary part of a healthy environment.

Glossary

antibiotic: A substance that kills or slows the growth of bacteria. Fungi produce some antibiotics.

cells: The basic building blocks of living organisms.

chitin: Chemical making up the cell wall of fungi and the hard skeleton of insects.

decomposer: An organism that feeds on the dead remains of other living things.

enzymes: Proteins that speed up a chemical reaction, like the breakdown of food.

fungicide: A chemical that kills fungi.

gills: Thin structures on the underside of a mushroom where spores grow.

hypha: (plural: hyphae) A long white thread of a fungus growing underground or in its food.

kingdom: The highest category into which living organisms are grouped.

lichen: An organism comprising a fungus and an alga living together.

mushroom: The fruiting body of some fungi.

mutualist: An organism that lives with another organism, where both benefit.

mycelium: (plural: mycelia) A mass of hyphae that make up the body of a fungus.

nutrients: A source of nourishment, including food and minerals.

parasite: An organism that lives on another organism and gets its food from its host.

penicillin: A kind of antibiotic that kills bacteria or slows bacterial growth.

pores: The openings on the underside of some fungi through which spores are released.

saprophyte: An organism that feeds on the dead remains of other living things.

spores: Reproductive cells made by fungi and certain other organisms that can grow into new organisms.

Books

Katya Arnold and Sam Swope, *Katya's Book of Mushrooms.* New York: Henry Holt, 1997. This book tells about hunting for mushrooms, where mushrooms grow, and how to identify different mushrooms.

Allan Fowler, *Good Mushrooms and Bad Toadstools.* Danbury, CT: Childrens Press, 1998. This easy-to-read book is about mushrooms that are good to eat and those that are poisonous.

Elaine Pascoe, *Slime Molds and Fungi.* Woodbridge, CT: Blackbirch Press, 1998. This book introduces fungi and slime molds and includes information about collecting fungi, growing molds, and experimenting to learn more about fungi. Colorful photographs bring fungi to life.

Jenny Tesar, *Fungi.* Woodbridge, CT: Blackbirch Press, 1994. This book provides an in-depth introduction to fungi, including information about the structure of fungi, how fungi react to their environment, how fungi get nourishment, and how fungi grow and reproduce. The role of fungi in the web of life is also discussed.

Internet Source

Robert Fogel, "Fun Facts About Fungi," updated May 14, 2003. www.herb.lsa.umich.edu/kidpage/factindx.htm.

Periodicals

Deborah Churchman, "Mushrooms: What a Wild Family!" *Ranger Rick*, September 2002. This article discusses what makes fungi, how fungi grow, and where to find them; it also explains several amazing fungi facts.

Gary Raham, "Lichens: Strange Plants with a Healthy Chemistry," *Cricket*, July 2000. This article introduces lichens, where they live, how they survive in hostile environments, and how their chemical properties help people.

Index

age, 9, 13
air pollution, 19
algae, 28
antibiotics, 36
ants, 28, 30
appearance, 4, 13
athlete's foot, 24

bird's nest fungi, 16–17
black mold, 21
bracket fungi, 10, 16
bread molds, 21

cells, 6–7
cellulose, 7
chestnut blight, 25–27
Chinese medicine, 37
chitin, 7
copper sulfate, 34
corn, 11
cyclosporins, 36

DeBary, Anton, 34
decomposers, 22–25
diabetes, 36
digestion, 9
diseases, 31–34

earthstars, 14, 16
enzymes, 9

fairy rings, 12–14
false morels, 19–20
Fleming, Alexander, 35–36
fruiting bodies
 of bracket fungi, 16
 dispersal of spores by, 11
 of earthstars, 14, 16
 mushrooms, 9–10
 of truffles, 19
fungicides, 24, 27
fungi "farmers," 28, 30

giant puffballs, 14
gills, 9–10

habitats, 4, 18
human diseases, 34
Hunt, Mary, 36
hyphae
 of algae, 28
 of bread mold, 21
 of fairy rings, 12
 of fungi on tree roots, 27–28
 growth of, 7–8
 leaf-cutting ants and, 28, 30
 of potato blight, 34
 spores and, 9
 of stinkhorn fungi, 17

insect pests, 27
Ireland, 33–34

Japanese medicine, 37

kingdoms, 6

leaf-cutting ants, 28, 30
lichens, 28
life span, 9, 13

medicines, 35–37
moisture, 21, 24
morels, 19–20
mushrooms, 9–10
  fairy rings and, 12–13
  wild, 19–20, 39
mutualists, 27–28, 38
mycelia, 8
  of fairy rings, 12–13
  of puffballs, 14
  spread of, 8–9
  of stinkhorn fungi, 17

Native Americans, 14
nuclei, 6

organ transplants, 36
oxygen, 23–24

parasites, 25–27, 32–34
penicillin, 35–36
Phytophthora infestans,
  33–34
plant diseases, 31–34
pollution, 19
potato blight, 33–34
potatoes, 32–34
preservation, 38
puffballs, 14

range, 4

recyclers, 22–25
reproduction. *See* spores
ringworm, 24
rust fungi, 31

saprophytes, 22–25
size, 4, 13
skin rashes, 24
smut, 11
species, number of, 6
spores, 9–11
  of bird's nest fungi, 16–17
  of earthstars, 16
  fairy rings and, 12
  of mold, 21
  of morels, 19
  of potato blight, 34
  of puffballs, 14
  of stinkhorn fungi, 17–18
  of truffles, 19
stinkhorn fungi, 17–18

temperatures, 24
trees, 25–28
tropical rain forests, 38
truffles, 18–19, 28

World War II, 36

yeasts, 20–21

Picture Credits

Cover: © PhotoDisc
© Art Today, Inc., 5, 30, 32, 40
© Sally Bensusen/Photo Researchers, Inc., 33
© Bettmann/CORBIS, 35, 37 (below)
© COREL Corporation, 10, 17, 24, 29, 39
© Michael & Patricia Fogden/CORBIS, 15
© Eric and David Hosking/CORBIS, 13
Chris Jouan, 8, 26
© Microfield Scientific Ltd./Photo Researchers, Inc., 20
© Outersurf.com, 23
© PhotoDisc, 7, 37 (inset)
© Adam Woolfitt/CORBIS, 18

Buffy Silverman searches for fungi growing near her home in Michigan. She is the author of *Genetics* for The KidHaven Science Library, and of two other books for young readers, *Bat's Night Out* and *Birds*. She has written many magazine stories for *Ladybug, Spider, Cricket, Highlights, Odyssey*, and *Ranger Rick*, and writes items for educational publishers and testing companies. She is also a writing instructor at the Institute of Children's Literature. Buffy shares her home with her husband, biologist Jeff Conner, and their children, Jake and Emma.